Better Homes a

Making CHRISTMAS DECORATIONS

RAGNHILD REES

MINI · WORKBOOK · SERIES

MURDOCH BOOKS®

Sydney • London • Vancouver • New York

CONTENTS

Patchwork balls and bells (top), ribbon wreath (far left) and the white and gold table (left)

This Christmas tree is both stylish and beautiful, and yet the decorations were simple to make and required no special skills.

Christmas decorations

How you decorate for Christmas depends very much on your personal taste, but the basic shapes of baubles and bells, stars and trees remain the same. The decorations in this book can be adapted to any style—just choose colours and fabrics to suit.

DECORATING TRADITIONS

There is a long history of decorating the house for Christmas. In Europe evergreen foliage such as holly and ivy symbolised eternal life and was associated with midwinter festivals back into pagan times. The Romans, for instance, decorated their houses for the Saturnalia festival (held around 25 December) with boughs and wreaths. Early Christians who wanted to avoid discovery continued this practice and so it became part of Christian tradition.

Today Christmas decorations are much more varied, although foliage garlands and wreaths remain an important element. Angels and stars, which play a part in the original story of Christmas, are an important feature, as are bells that ring out the glad tidings. For many people a Nativity scene is an essential reminder of the meaning of Christmas and a centrepiece of their seasonal decorations. Bright baubles and stockings for gifts are more recent additions to the range.

Different countries have added particular decorations to the tradition, for example the Christmas tree first took its present form in Germany during the sixteenth century, while the glowing advent star on page 42 is a traditional Scandinavian window decoration.

CREATING YOUR STYLE

When planning your Christmas decorations, choose a style that fits in with your existing decor and suits the climate. Most important for the result will be your choice of colour scheme, and the projects in this book have been designed to look equally attractive in any colour.

● Glittering white and gold is always elegant. This combination can suggest snowy winter landscapes or give a light, summery feel in the southern hemisphere.

● A traditional atmosphere can be created with lots of red and green, and images of snow. This is a style that goes back to Victorian times.

● A similar cosy but rather more sophisticated result comes from the use of rich jewel-like colours and lots of gold.

● A modern, stylish effect can be achieved by using a single pale colour such as apricot or pink for your base. Silver makes an effective foil for such colours.

Beaded bells

These exquisite bells are made by winding beaded wire around a mould and 'sewing' it together with more wires. If carefully stored they'll last for many Christmases.

MAKING THE BELL SHAPE

1 Cut a piece of 26-gauge wire 3.2 m long. Wrap a piece of masking tape around the wire about 5 cm from one end.

2 Thread seed beads onto the wire until you have about 3 m of beaded wire. Secure temporarily with tape.

3 Remove the tape and make a circle with the first eight seed beads. Push the wire through the first bead or around the wire between the beads to secure it. Bend the beaded wire around this inner circle to form a double circle for the top of the bell.

4 Cut four 30 cm pieces of 28-gauge wire. Tape them together for 10 cm from one end. Place this bundle through the centre of the beaded circle, with the taped end projecting at the top. These wires will be used to 'sew' the bell together. Take one wire at a time and bend it around the two circles from underneath and around over the top. Space the wires evenly around the circle so that the circles are joined in four places. Use the pliers to tighten the wire. Push the beads close together as you work the bell.

MATERIALS FOR BELLS

- Medium-size seed beads: gold, silver, red, pale blue and dark blue
- One 14 mm bead in matching colour for each bell
- One 8 mm bead in matching colour for each bell
- Three 14 inch (35.5 cm) lengths of 24-gauge wire for each bell
- 26-gauge beading wire
- 28-gauge beading wire
- Wire cutters or a pair of old scissors
- Masking tape
- Small flat-nosed pliers
- Polystyrene bell shape 7 cm high
- Cord for hanging
- Pencil

5 Cut all the 24-gauge wire to 4 cm lengths. Bend each into a U-shape. These U-pins hold the beaded wire in place while the bell is constructed.

6 Use the pencil to draw four lines on the polystyrene bell from top to bottom so that it is divided into four equal parts. Place the beaded circle on top of the bell and secure it with U-pins. Working in a clockwise direction, wrap the beaded wire around the bell to the first mark.

Glittering beaded bells will give a sumptuous touch to your Christmas decorations. To make the beaded monograms, see page 58.

Seed beads and one 14 mm bead are threaded on wire to make the clapper.

Take one of the four wires from underneath and wrap it around the beaded wire. Always take the wire from underneath and wrap it over the top—if you wrap from the top you will have to go around twice and this makes the wrapping bulky. Tighten with the pliers. Continue around the bell, wrapping at each of the marked lines. Secure with U-pins as needed.

TO FINISH

7 Remove the bell from the mould. Finish it by taking the wrapping wires through the beads in front or by wrapping them neatly around the beaded wire. Cut off the excess wire.

8 To make the clapper, cut a 35 cm piece of 26-gauge wire. Place one seed bead in the centre and fold the wire in half. Thread both ends through a 14 mm bead and then through seed beads until the clapper is the right length. Place the clapper inside the bell so that the wires come through the top of the bell. Twist these wires around the four wrapping wires a few times, and then trim away three of the four wrapping wires. There will then be three wires. Remove any tape left and thread on the top 8 mm bead. Twist the wires together to make a loop. Insert the wires back into the bead and secure before trimming off excess wire.

9 Place a piece of cord in the loop for hanging.

HINT

If you want all the bells to be the same size make no more than three from the same mould. The polystyrene will be compressed as you work so that each subsequent bell will be a fraction smaller.

---

6 Wrap the beaded wire around the bell, securing it with the four wires and U-pins as you go.

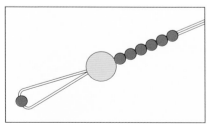

8 To make the clapper, add one seed bead, fold the wire in half then add the clapper bead and more seed beads.

Glittering stars

These simple gold stars are made very quickly and have many uses. Careful cutting is the key to a neat finish.

MATERIALS

- Screenboard, 900 UMS
- Gold spray paint
- Gold glitter
- Pencil and tracing paper
- Scalpel and cutting mat
- Metal ruler
- Glue pen
- Large needle
- Gold cord for hanging

These glittering stars make ideal window decorations, or small ones can be used to decorate a table or tree, or even as gift tags.

METHOD

1 Enlarge the pattern on page 60 on a photocopier or draw it yourself. The window stars are 12.5 cm across; the table stars on page 52 are 10.5 cm.

2 With the pencil and tracing paper, trace the pattern on the screenboard. Cut out the star using the scalpel, metal ruler and cutting mat.

3 Spray the star with the gold paint. Make sure it is dry before turning it over to spray the other side.

4 With the glue pen, draw around the edges of the front and sprinkle a generous amount of glitter on top. Let it dry and then shake off the excess. If desired, add glitter to the other side of the star.

5 Use the needle to make a small hole between two points of the star. Thread the needle with a gold cord and pass it through the star. Knot the ends together ready for hanging.

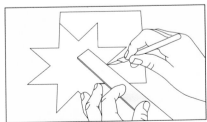

2 Transfer the star design to the screenboard and cut out the shape using the scalpel and metal ruler.

Painted glass balls will make a brilliant addition to any Christmas tree. The 'leadlight' designs used on these balls recall the stained glass designs used in traditional church windows.

Painted glass balls

These painted glass balls will add a rich and lustrous touch to your tree, and they're not difficult to make using the 'rubber band' method described here.

METHOD

1 Place two elastic bands around the face of the glass ball, to one side of the hanging point, so they make a wide, even band.

2 With the pen, draw a line on both sides of the elastic bands to make the outline for the edging band (see the patterns on page 13).

3 Reposition the elastic bands to find the centre line going from north (the hanging point) to south. Draw this line. Reposition the bands to find the centre line from east to west and draw in this line. Reposition the bands to find the centre (diagonal) lines between. On each diagonal line, mark a point 1.5 cm from the centre. Following the desired pattern, draw in the remaining lines.

MATERIALS

- Glass balls, approximately 8.5 cm in diameter
- Glass paint (solvent-based): red, green, yellow, blue
- Relief paint: black
- Wide elastic bands
- Fine felt-tipped permanent pen
- Cotton buds
- Glass (to hold ball)
- Paint brush: no.3
- White spirit

4 Place the ball in a glass for support and, using the relief paint, draw evenly over the lines. Leave to dry.

5 Remove any pen marks still showing with a damp cotton bud. They come off the glass quite easily.

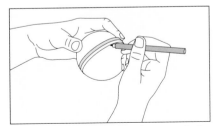

1 Place two rubber bands around the face of the glass ball to one side of the hanging point to create an even band.

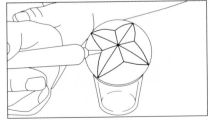

4 Place the ball in a glass for support and, using the relief paint, draw evenly over the lines. Leave it to dry.

Black relief paint outlines the coloured panels to achieve the 'leadlight' effect.

6 Paint the coloured panels using a dabbing motion. If you think that the paint is not strong enough, go over it again before it dries: this creates a textured look. Start with the yellow star and all other yellow sections. Let this paint dry before going on to the next colour. Clean the brush with white spirit between colours. Complete the painting and place the ball in a glass to dry.

6 Paint the coloured panels using a dabbing motion, cleaning the brush thoroughly between colours.

USING RELIEF PAINT

- Before starting clean the glass to make sure it is grease-free.
- Practise using relief paint on paper to ensure you'll get a line that is of a consistent thickness.
- Keep the nozzle of the relief paint clean to avoid blobs, and always replace the cap after use to prevent the paint hardening.
- Use a firm, smooth movement when drawing the lines.
- Start drawing at the top left-hand corner (right-hand if you're left-handed) and work down to avoid smudging your work.
- Make sure the relief paint is completely dry before filling in the panels or it will bleed into the coloured panels.

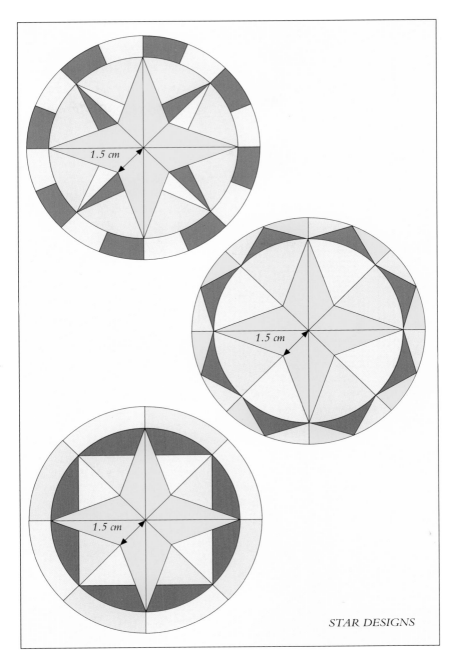

STAR DESIGNS

Miniature stockings

Three different Christmas designs are used for these little stockings worked in cross stitch on Aida fabric. They can be hung on the tree as they are or a treat could be popped inside.

MATERIALS

- White 14-count Aida 40 x 30 cm
- DMC stranded embroidery cottons: red (321), blue (799), yellow (743), green (319) and brown (420)
- Cardboard
- Water soluble pen
- Tapestry needle size 26
- Scissors
- Pins
- Sewing thread
- Sewing machine (optional)
- Pencil

METHOD

1 Enlarge the pattern on page 16 by 200 per cent on a photocopier and make a template from cardboard. Transfer the shape onto the Aida with the water soluble pen. Reverse the pattern to outline a piece for the back. Leave at least 1 cm around each shape but don't cut them out.

2 Embroider the designs using two strands of cotton and working each stitch over one square. Beginning one square below the fold line, work two rows of cross stitch in alternate squares as a border. Then, following the charts on page 17, embroider the designs, starting the candle and tree six squares below the border and the bauble fifteen squares below. Work the cross stitch first and then the back and straight stitches.

3 Cut out the stocking shapes, leaving a 6 mm seam allowance except at the top. Place a front and a back together, right sides facing, and pin. Stitch around the stocking sides and bottom with a machine or by hand. Trim the seam and snip into the seam at the top of the foot. Turn right side out. Fold down at the fold line and slip stitch in place. Remove any pen marks with a damp cloth.

4 To make the twisted cord, take 1 m of red stranded cotton. Double it and knot the ends together. Place the cotton over a nail, hook or

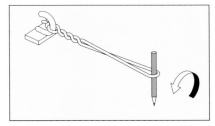

4 Place the cotton over a nail or similar object. Place a pencil at one end and twirl the cotton until tight.

These cross-stitched stockings would suit a traditional Christmas tree and they're very easy to stitch. Use a candle, bauble or tiny Christmas tree for your stockings—or stitch them all.

The neat cross stitches on these stockings are enhanced by the use of back and straight stitches to produce these lovely little stockings.

similar object. Place a pencil at the other end and twirl the cotton until tight. Lift the twisted cotton off the nail, holding the ends together. Tie the ends together.

5 Attach the twisted cord in a loop to the back of the stocking with a few stitches.

6 Place the stocking on a soft underlayer and iron.

HINT
Use these designs to decorate other Christmas items, such as table napkins or place cards, greeting cards or gift tags.

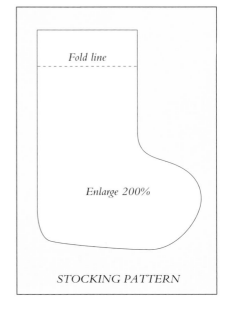

Fold line

Enlarge 200%

STOCKING PATTERN

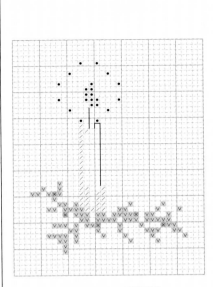

CANDLE DESIGN

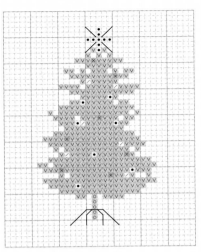

TREE DESIGN

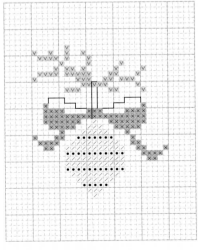

BAUBLE DESIGN

Colour key

☒	Red
•	Yellow
╱	Blue
⋁	Green
⊙	Brown

Back stitch:
Candle: blue and wick brown
Bauble: bow red and hanging blue
Tree: stand green

Straight stitch:
Tree: star yellow

These patchwork balls and bells will add a special touch to a tree decorated in elegant silver and pastels, but if you prefer they can be made in red, green and gold for a more traditional look.

Patchwork balls and bells

Pale, cool colours are combined with silver lamé to make these lovely patchwork balls and bells. Pearl-studded ribbons cover the joins and add a sophisticated touch.

MATERIALS

- Four polystyrene balls 7.5 cm in diameter
- Two polystyrene bells 7 cm high
- 20 cm pale blue cotton fabric
- 20 cm pale green cotton fabric
- 20 cm silver lamé fabric
- 1 m of 4 mm wide silver ribbon for each ball or bell
- Silver pearl beads
- Two round bells for clappers
- Paper streamer
- Glass-topped pins and plain pins
- Pencil
- Rubber
- Aluminium foil
- Scissors
- Scalpel
- Nail file

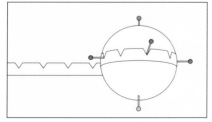

2 Take Ball 1 and position the paper streamer around the Equator to find and mark the lines.

MARKING THE DESIGN

1 To mark out the patchwork design on the balls and bells, use a paper streamer and pins. Place one end of the paper streamer on a ball (or the top of the bell) and fix it with a glass-headed pin. This becomes the North Pole for that ball. Wrap the paper around the ball back to the North Pole and cut it close to the pin. Fold the paper in half and use it to measure off the South Pole on the ball. Mark it with a pin of a different colour. Fold the paper in half again to find the Equator line and mark it around the ball with pins of a different colour. Cut the top corners off the folded paper so that the pins can be placed accurately in the centre of the paper strip (see the step diagram on this page). By moving the marker and placing pins in the appropriate place you will be able to create many different designs.

THE BALLS

2 Using the streamer method and a pencil, mark the designs (see page 21) on the balls. Ball 1 is divided into eight equal parts. Draw a line around the ball through the North and South poles. Use the paper strip around the Equator to find and mark

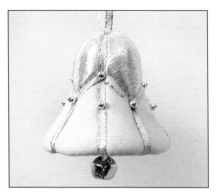

The silver ribbons are held in place with pearl-topped pins.

the other lines. Divide Balls 2, 3 and 4 into four equal parts by drawing a line around the ball through the poles and another around the Equator. Complete the designs, using the measurements given on the diagrams. Rub out unwanted lines.

3 Make a pattern for each section of the design by placing a piece of foil on top of the section. Bend the foil to fit the shape, then cut it out.

4 Place the foil pattern on the fabric and cut out the shape with a 1 cm seam allowance.

5 With a scalpel, make cuts along the marked lines. Place the piece of fabric on top of the section and push the edges of the fabric into the ball with a nail file. Finish each section before moving to the next.

6 When all the fabric has been added, cover the joins with ribbon.

Pull the ribbon tight and at each intersection fix it in place with a plain pin onto which a silver pearl bead has been threaded. Cover as many of the joins as possible with one length of ribbon, then cut the ribbon and sink the end into the ball. Start the new length the same way, holding it in place with a pearled pin.

7 Make a hanging loop with 20 cm of ribbon. Fold the ribbon into a loop and pin it in place.

THE BELLS

8 The bells are made in the same way except for the base. Draw a circle around the base 6–8 mm in from the edge and cut it. Bring the fabric around the edge and push it into the circle.

9 Place the ribbon over the joins as for the balls but finish all the ribbon ends in the centre of the base. Make one length of ribbon a little longer. Thread a round metal bell onto this ribbon for the clapper. Place a plain pin either side of the clapper to hold it in place.

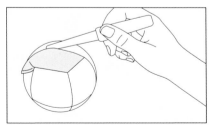

5 Place the fabric on top of the section and push the edges into the ball with a nail file.

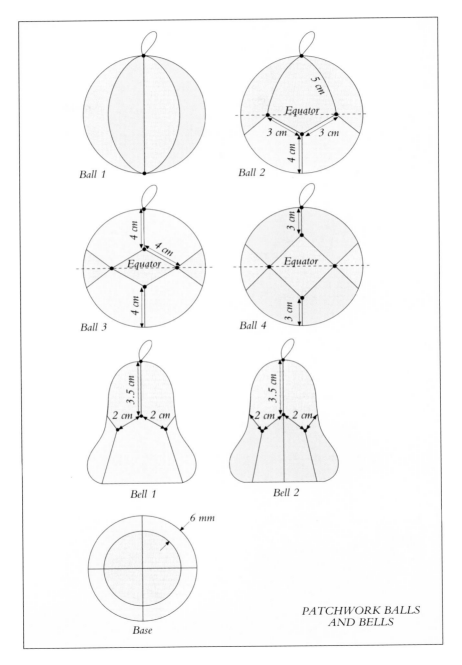

Ball 1

Ball 2

5 cm

Equator

3 cm   3 cm

4 cm

Ball 3

4 cm

4 cm

Equator

4 cm

Ball 4

3 cm

Equator

3 cm

Bell 1

3.5 cm

2 cm   2 cm

Bell 2

3.5 cm

2 cm   2 cm

Base

6 mm

PATCHWORK BALLS
AND BELLS

Advent tree

These delightful organza bags make an original alternative to a traditional Advent calendar. They look splendid on a tree, whether on your Christmas tree or a special Advent tree.

MAKING THE BAG

1 Cut the organza ribbon into 40 cm lengths. Fold in each end of each piece 6 cm and pin.

2 Stitch across the ribbon 1 cm from the raw edge. Stitch again 1 cm above the first row to make a casing.

3 Fold the ribbon in half with right sides together and the top folds aligned. Pin the sides together from the base to the lower casing seam. Sew the two side seams to the casing seam; fasten off. Turn right side out.

4 Thread the needle with 40 cm of the gold yarn and thread it through both casings, ending at the starting side. Knot the cord about 3 cm out. Repeat from the other side of the casing with another piece of yarn.

MATERIALS

- 2.40 m of 10 cm wide organza ribbon in each of red, gold, navy and light blue
- Scissors and pins
- Sewing machine
- Sewing threads to match the organza
- Tapestry needle size 18
- Gold knitting yarn
- Thin card, 160 g
- Pencil and tracing paper
- Number stickers or stencils 13 mm high (1–24)

ADDING THE LABEL

5 Trace the heart pattern on page 60. Make a template of the shape and cut out twenty-four hearts from the card. Place a number sticker on each heart, near the lower end, or stencil the numbers onto the hearts.

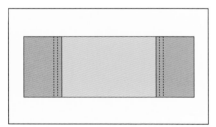

2 Stitch across the ribbon 1 cm from the raw edge and then stitch a second row to make a casing.

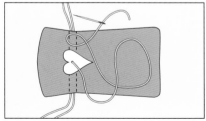

6 Catch the fabric on either side of the casing and push the needle through the heart.

Fine organza ribbon is used for these beautiful little bags. Opening each one to find the treat inside will be a highlight of the days leading up to Christmas.

6 Thread the needle with a very long piece of gold yarn. Take one bag and, with the opening facing you, use the needle to pick up a thread or two of fabric on the casing seam, then a bit on the other seam. Avoid the pulling cord. Then push the needle through the heart from the wrong side about 0.5 cm from the top. Pull the yarn through, knot and make a small bow. Cut the yarn. Repeat for all the other bags.

7 Place a treat in each bag and close it, bringing the cords to the centre through the side splits in the frill.

The conical shape of this fine angel allows it to fit neatly over the top of the tree and sit there steadily. All you need to make it are cardboard, spray paint and sharp scissors.

Angel tree topper

This charming gold angel is made entirely from card and is cut out in one piece. It makes an effective tree topper or will sit on a mantelpiece or sideboard.

METHOD

1 Enlarge the pattern on page 60 on a photocopier by 200 per cent. Using the pencil, trace the pattern onto tracing paper and transfer it to the wrong side of the card.

2 With the scissors, first cut around the outline of the pattern and then cut the inside lines and 'arms'.

3 Spray paint the card on both sides. Allow it to dry.

4 Fold the 'arms' down and forward.

5 To assemble the angel and create the wings, place cut line A into cut line B.

MATERIALS

- Slightly textured white card, 250 g
- Gold spray paint
- Tracing paper
- Pencil
- Small pair of scissors

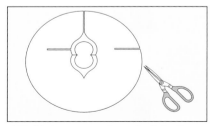

4 Fold the cut-out 'arms' of the figure down and forward to free the round shape of the head.

RIBBON BOWS

Ribbon bows are simple yet elegant decorations that will suit most Christmas trees (see pages 4 and 18). The diagram below shows the correct way to tie a bow so that it looks neat and symmetrical when finished.

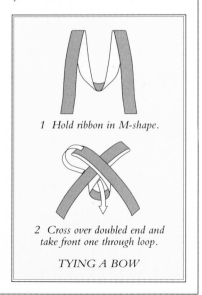

1 Hold ribbon in M-shape.

2 Cross over doubled end and take front one through loop.

TYING A BOW

Leaf garland

Natural leaves are wired to a paper twist to form this garland which can be made into any shape desired. Ribbons decorate the loops from which it is securely hung.

MATERIALS

- Brown paper twist, 5.40 m long (for a garland 2.25 m long)
- 90–100 natural holly oak leaves
- 14 inch (35.5 cm) long 22-gauge wires
- Reel of 24-gauge wire
- Wire cutters and scissors
- Brown florists tape
- 1.60 m of 5 cm wide ribbon

METHOD

1 Push one 22-gauge wire into a leaf about 1.5 cm from the stem until the leaf is in the centre of the wire. Fold the wire into a U-shape, then twist the top wire tightly a couple of times around the stem and then around the other wire. Repeat this for the rest of the leaves.

2 Tear off a length of florists tape and pull it about 2–3 cm from the end. This part will become thin and transparent and will stick to itself. Take one leaf and place the tape on the wires. Twist the tape around the wires to secure. Tape over the entire wires, pulling the tape 2–3 cm at a time with your left hand and twisting the wire with the right. If the tape breaks, put it back on the wire and

pull and twist. Complete all the leaves. (If you have not used florists tape before, practise on a length of wire before tackling the leaves.)

3 For the base fold the paper twist in half. Wire it together 9–10 cm from the fold to create a loop. Place the loop on a door handle and twist one end around the other. Make a loop at the other end. Cover the wires with a bit of florists tape.

4 Start attaching leaves in the centre of the twist, using the 24-gauge reel wire. Secure one leaf, then place another in front of it and leaning to the left so it covers the base of the first leaf. Then secure one leaning to the right. Take the wire around each leaf twice and incorporate the wires from the leaf in front each time. Work to the end and then from the centre to the other end.

5 Cut an 80 cm length of ribbon. Tie a bow (see page 25) with tails about 12 cm long. Turn the bow so the tails are at the back. Place a covered wire in the centre of the bow and secure it to one end of the garland to cover the wire ends. Repeat at the other end.

A leafy garland can be used to decorate a mantelpiece, wall or staircase and will suit most styles of Christmas decor.

1 Push the wire end into the leaf about 1.5 cm from the stem until the leaf is in the centre of the wire.

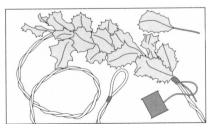

4 Attach the leaves to the paper twist, taking the reel wire around each leaf twice to secure it.

These delicate snowflakes are inspired by traditional European Christmas decorations but their glittering beauty will appeal anywhere in the world.

Glass snowflakes

Made from glass beads threaded on wire, these lovely snowflakes will look wonderful hanging in a window or on a tree. Make each slightly different as no two snowflakes are the same.

MATERIALS (FOR 1)

- Large, clear seed beads
- Two flat-sided diamanté beads
- Clear glass beads, six each of three or four types
- Two 22-gauge wires
- Piece of scrap card
- Blu-Tack and tape
- General purpose clear adhesive
- Wire cutters or old scissors
- Clothes peg
- Small round-nosed pliers
- 3 kg fishing line

METHOD

1 Place a piece of Blu-Tack on the card. Press one diamanté lightly into the Blu-Tack. Put a piece of Blu-Tack about 8 cm from the centre at 12, 2, 4, 6, 8 and 10 o'clock. These pieces will support the wires.

2 Put a generous amount of adhesive on the diamanté. Cut a wire 18 cm long and place the centre of the wire in the centre of the diamanté at 12 o'clock. This will be the hanging wire so mark it with a bit of tape. Cut four wires 10 cm long and place them on the diamanté at 2, 4, 8 and 10 o'clock. Put on more adhesive and place another diamanté on top, aligning the holes. Leave to dry for about 30 minutes, and then put a peg on the diamanté centre. If you move the shape too early, it will fall apart. Leave to cure for 24 hours.

3 Remove the peg. Work on one prong at a time. Thread on the beads, placing a seed bead first and between each larger bead. The finished length of each prong should be no more than 5 cm or the snowflake will be too heavy.

4 Cut the wire 1 cm from the last bead. Using the pliers, turn the end of the wire into a circle. Don't tighten it too much or you may pull the wire out of its socket. Tie fishing line through the circle on the hanging wire.

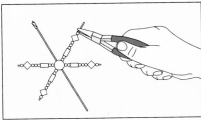

4 Cut the wire 1 cm from the last bead and use the pliers to turn the end of the wire into a circle.

The three kings

Kings Balthazar, Melchior and Casper are an integral part of the Christmas story. They are created here with stiffened fabric and glass beads and their caskets of myrrh, gold and frankincense are in the shape of fruits.

MATERIALS

- 1.50 m natural plain cheesecloth
- Three polystyrene cones 8 cm in diameter and 20 cm high
- Three polystyrene balls 5 cm in diameter
- Scalpel
- General purpose clear adhesive
- Tape measure
- Scissors
- Paper and pencil (for pattern)
- Fabric stiffener
- Plastic container (for stiffener)
- Strong thread
- Glue gun
- Fleece (cream, white and brown)
- Three chenille pipe cleaners

- Six oval wooden beads
- Large purple glass bead
- Twenty-four clear seed beads
- Twenty-six clear bugle beads
- Twelve gold saucer beads
- Four large gold seed beads
- Thirty-six small gold seed beads
- Pins
- Three wooden fruit shapes (two pears and an acorn)
- Three tiny wooden beads
- Artists acrylic paints: gold, purple and moss green
- Paint brush
- Varnish (optional)

THE BASIC FIGURES

1 Take one polystyrene cone and, if it has a point, use the scalpel to trim off 2 cm. Some cones have a flat top and the head sits neatly without trimming. Using the clear adhesive, glue a polystyrene ball to the cone. Let dry. Repeat for the other figures.

2 Measure the figure from the base, across the head and down the other

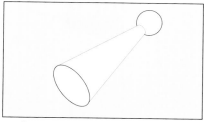

1 If the polystyrene cone has a point, trim it off and glue a polystyrene ball to the cone to form the basic shape.

Each of the three kings has his own characteristics: King Casper has a crown and a brown beard, King Melchior a jewelled crown and long white beard and King Balthazar a turban with purple jewel. For the leaf garland see page 26.

The crowns consist of beaded pins placed evenly around the head.

cone. Tie tightly around the neck with the thread. Don't worry about any wrinkles on the head, for these kings are old men. Now bring folds from the sides to the front to create an illusion of a coat over the dress. Arrange the back neatly. Dip a rectangular piece of fabric in the fabric stiffener as before. Fold the long sides to the centre and fold again. Wrap it around the head like a turban. Casper's turban is also wrapped around his neck.

side with the tape measure. Cut a circle of fabric with this measurement as the diameter. Cut another piece of fabric 36 x 15 cm for the turban. Enlarge the pattern for the sleeves opposite on a photocopier at 200 per cent and make a paper pattern. Cut out the sleeves.

3 Dilute the fabric stiffener with water to a runny consistency. Place one circle of fabric in the container and stir it around. Wring it out as you would wet clothes. Place the centre of the fabric on top of one figure and smooth it down the front onto the

4 Open out the sleeve fabric and place it in the fabric stiffener as before. Lay it flat, place a pipe cleaner on the fold line and fold the fabric over it. Don't cut the pipe cleaner at this stage. Leave the fabric to dry a little before placing the sleeves on the shoulder. Arrange the sleeves, keeping them in place with a pin. When they are dry, use a glue gun to secure them properly. Cut the pipe cleaners to fit the oval wooden beads and glue the beads on to form hands.

5 Leave the figures to dry for about 24 hours, then trim the coats.

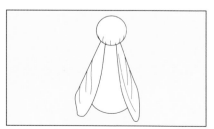

3 Place the fabric on the figure, tie it around the neck and bring folds from the sides to create the 'coat'.

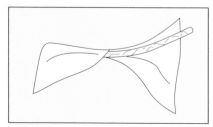

4 To make the sleeves, place a pipe cleaner in the centre of the fabric and fold the fabric over it.

THE ATTRIBUTES

6 Glue the purple bead to the centre of King Balthazar's turban and glue cream fleece to his chin to form a short beard. Give King Melchior a long white beard and King Casper a short brown one.

7 Add the crowns.

• King Melchior's crown consists of sixteen pins placed in a circle on the head. Thread four pins each with two clear seed beads, one gold saucer bead and two clear seed beads. Place them at 12, 6, 3 and 9 o'clock. Thread another four pins with a gold saucer bead, a bugle bead and a saucer bead and place them midway between the other pins. A pin with one seed bead is placed between each of these pins.

• King Casper's crown consists of four pins each threaded with a tiny gold bead and a clear bugle bead, repeated three times. Place them at 12, 3, 6 and 9 o'clock. Thread four other pins with two small gold beads, one large gold bead and two small gold beads. Place them midway between the first four pins. Place a pin with a small gold bead on it between each pin.

8 Glue the small wooden beads to the fruit shapes to form 'stems'. Paint one pear purple, the other moss green. Paint the acorn and the stems gold. Allow the fruit 'caskets' to dry, then varnish them if desired.

9 Use the glue gun to glue the hands together, then glue the caskets above the joined hands.

HINT

The three kings make a stylish Christmas decoration but an entire Nativity scene could be produced from the same basic figures. Wrap a shawl around Mary's head and give her a swaddled baby Jesus to hold, and give the shepherds crooks.

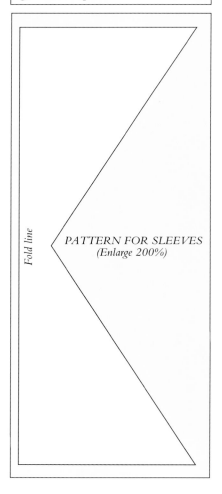

Fold line

PATTERN FOR SLEEVES
(Enlarge 200%)

This delicate angel chain can be hung across a window, in a Christmas tree or on a mantelpiece, but do take care if you light the fire! To make the standing angels, see the instructions on page 25.

Angel paper chain

This row of dainty angels is a contemporary version of traditional paper chains. The basic technique is simple and all you need to re-create them is the design and sharp scissors.

METHOD

1 Cut a piece of wrapping paper 1.12 m long and 20 cm wide.

2 Fold it in half and then in half again. Repeat until the paper is only 7 cm wide.

3 Using the pencil, transfer the pattern (see page 60) to the folded paper, placing the centre line against the folded edge of the paper.

4 With the scissors cut out the shape, starting at the top of the head and

working around the top of the wing. Leave the area near the top of the wing where the figures join and cut around the lower part of the figure. Do not tug at the paper: keep snipping until it comes away easily.

5 Unfold the angels and hang them up with Blu-Tack.

4 With the scissors cut out the shape. Do not tug at the paper: keep snipping until it comes away easily.

PAPER DECORATIONS

Christmas decorations made from paper are part of childhood memories, but their clean lines and simple shapes give them a place in many modern decorative schemes too.

Whatever your project, a few basic rules will ensure that you achieve a good result.

- Ensure any fold lines are clean and sharp.
- Use small, pointed scissors or a sharp craft knife and cutting mat. The scissors or knife should be very sharp.
- Always draw the pattern on the reverse of the item as it is difficult to erase pencil marks.
- Always cut precisely into corners and don't try to tug out pieces as the design may tear.

Peppercorn wreath

For this seasonal wreath peppercorns were wired to a twig backing and sprayed with florists paint to enhance their colour. The wreath was finished with varnish to preserve the effect.

MATERIALS

- Wreath backing 25 cm in diameter
- One large bunch of peppercorns
- 14 inch (35.5 cm) long 22-gauge wires
- Brown florists tape
- Wire cutters or old scissors
- Florists spray paint: cranberry (optional)
- Small flat-nosed pliers
- Spray varnish
- Fishing line

METHOD

1 Divide the peppercorns into small bunches with about three stems in each bunch. Fold one wire in half with a loop in the centre. Place the loop at the back of a bunch and twist one end of the wire around the stems and the other end of the wire. Make a few tight turns. Twist the two wires together. Wire all bunches.

2 Cover all the wired stems with florists tape. (If you have not used it before, practise on a length of wire before tackling the peppercorns.) Tear off a length of tape and pull it about 2–3 cm from the end. This part will become thin and transparent and will stick to itself. Place the tape on the wires of one bunch, twist a bit to secure it and then twist the wire with your right hand. Pull the tape 2–3 cm at a time with your left hand, and twist with the right until you need to pull the tape again. If the tape breaks, put it back on the wire and pull and twist as before.

3 Cover a few extra wires with tape and cut in half. Combine three bunches in a fan shape. Wire them together using a half wire. Cut the wire stems to 5 cm. Make 12–13 large bunches. If desired, spray the peppercorns with florists paint to get a stronger colour.

4 Cover more wires with florists tape (two for each bunch). Place a bunch of peppercorns at the centre top of the wreath. Take a covered wire and place it on the neck of the bunch and around the wreath backing. Twist it together and tighten with pliers. Place a second wire on this bunch and tighten as before. Repeat with other bunches, spacing them so that the whole base is covered.

5 Spray varnish the finished wreath. Tie on fishing line for hanging.

The relaxed outline of this wreath adds interest to the simple shape and the red colour gives a traditional Christmas touch.

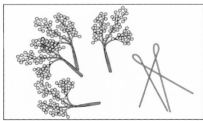

1 Divide the peppercorns into small bunches and fold wires in half with a loop in the centre.

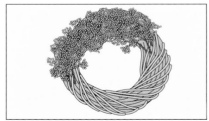

4 Wire the peppercorn bunches to the wreath base, spacing them so that the whole base is covered.

These lovely stockings are definitely for adults and will help any jaded reveller recapture the excitement of Christmas morning.

Christmas stockings

Stockings decorated with ribbon weaving can be as bright or as mellow as you like. Threads are drawn from the evenweave fabric and then the ribbons are woven through.

MATERIALS (FOR 1 STOCKING)★

- Cream Zweigart Lugana cloth 50 x 30 cm
- 80 cm of 6–8 different ribbons, in different widths, no more than 2 cm wide
- Embroidery cotton to match ribbons (optional)
- 40 cm interfacing
- 40 cm cream satin fabric
- 40 cm cream lining fabric
- Water soluble pen
- Scissors
- Tapestry needle size 18
- Pins
- 1.50 m piping
- Sewing machine
- Sewing thread

★ Or 50 x 69 cm Lugana for three stockings. The satin, lining and interfacing will be enough for three.

MAKING THE FRONT

1 Enlarge the pattern on page 41 using the grid. Transfer the shape to fabric with a water soluble pen. Cut out, adding 4 cm seam allowance.

2 Starting from the edge of the fabric and 4 cm down from the fold line, pull out enough threads to accommodate the width of the first ribbon. Thread the tapestry needle with the ribbon, then push the point of the needle through the end of the ribbon and pull tight. This leaves no tail to be pulled through the work and makes it easier to thread the ribbon through the fabric. Decide how many threads of the fabric to leave between each weave of the ribbon. This should be consistent over the row and should vary from row to row. Weave the ribbon in and out across the front.

3 Leave varying numbers of threads between each ribbon row. Continue weaving until the stocking front is covered. Using embroidery cotton add rows of running stitch between the ribbons as desired.

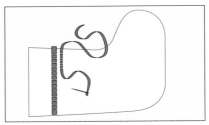

2 *Weave the ribbon in and out across the front, working over and under a consistent number of threads.*

Piping to match the ribbons provides a neat finish for these stockings.

4 When the ribbon weaving is completed, pin the piping around the pen line on the right side of the shape, except across the top, with all raw edges facing outwards. Cut out a matching stocking front from the interfacing and pin it against the wrong side of the shape. Machine stitch around the stocking.

5 Remove the cord from the piping from the top to the fold line. This eliminates bulk. Turn the pattern over and cut out another stocking shape in interfacing and one in satin for the back.

6 Pin the satin and interfacing together and place them on the ribbon woven stocking, right sides together. Tack them together and then sew, using the stitch line as a guide. Trim the seams close to the stitching line. Turn right sides out.

7 Pin the piping on the fold line around the top of the stocking, starting from the back seam. Remove the cord inside the piping where it overlaps. Tack and stitch in place. Fold the top in along the fold line.

ASSEMBLING THE STOCKING

8 Draw the stocking shape on the lining fabric with the water soluble pen. Cut out two pieces. Pin together with right sides facing and sew 0.5 cm inside the lines to enable the lining to fit. Trim the seams.

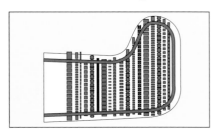

4 Pin the piping around the pen line, except at the top of the stocking, with all raw edges facing outwards.

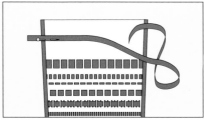

7 Pin the piping on the fold line around the top of the stocking. Start pinning from the back seam.

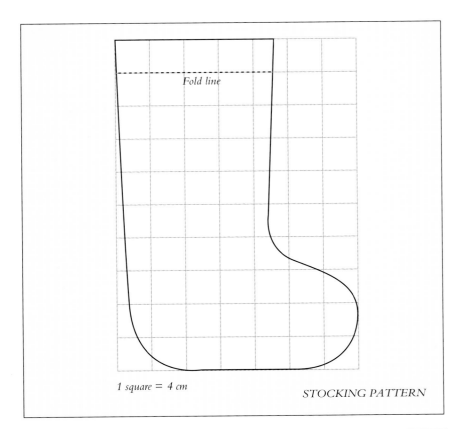

Fold line

1 square = 4 cm

STOCKING PATTERN

Fold down the top of the lining to the fold line.

9 Cut a length of ribbon, fold it in half and stitch it securely into the back of the stocking to make a hanging loop.

10 Insert the lining in the stocking. Pin it in place and slip stitch around the top.

11 If any pen marks still show, remove them with a damp cloth.

HINT

Ribbon woven stockings can be made in any size. For example, miniature versions make wonderful tree decorations.

For miniature stockings use the pattern without enlarging it and weave in 4–6 mm wide ribbons. As with the larger stockings you can use embroidery cottons and running stitch to provide variety. The piping may be omitted or folded ribbon used in its place.

Advent star

Welcome family and friends with this traditional Scandinavian window decoration. Light from an electric light bulb glows through the holes punched in the paper star.

MATERIALS

- White paper, 160 g
- Screenboard, 900 UMS
- Large sheet of scrap paper
- One-hole puncher
- Metal ruler
- Scalpel
- Double-sided tape
- Pencil and tracing paper
- Clips for holding star together (Nalclip, small)
- Light fitting, plug and electrical wire
- 15W pilot light bulb
- Clips or hooks for hanging star
- Screwdriver
- Cutting mat
- Correction fluid or white paint

MAKING THE POINTS

1 Enlarge the patterns on page 45 by 400 per cent on a photocopier (200 per cent twice). Transfer the star points to the wrong side of the paper. There will be seven points. Add all the crease lines.

2 Cut out the star points, using the scalpel, metal ruler and the cutting mat. Make the small cut between the tabs at the bottom of Point A.

3 Take one Point A and fold the long tab on the left side on the marked crease line. Take the untabbed side, line it up on top of the tab to find the centre line, and crease in place. Open it up and fold the untabbed side to the middle. Crease in place. With it still folded, fold it again and then fold the tabbed side over it and crease in the final line. Fold the other tabs. Repeat for the rest of the star points.

4 Place the first point on a piece of scrap paper. Put double-sided tape on the tabs, on the right side of the paper. Hold it to a window (this makes it easier to see) and cut off the excess. Do not remove the tape cover at this stage. Repeat for all star points.

5 Remove the tape cover from the long tab on the left side and place the

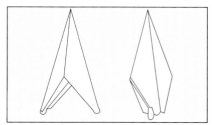

5 Place the untabbed side on top of the tab so the point looks like a bird's beak. Fold it back so it lies flat.

This luminous seven-point star will brighten your Christmas windows. It isn't too difficult to make and, once dismantled, it can be folded flat and stored from year to year.

untabbed side on top. The point will look a bit like a bird's beak. Fold it back the other way so it lies perfectly flat (so the star can be folded flat when not in use). Repeat for the other points.

6 Take one point and refold so the join is in the centre again. Using the hole puncher, make a row of holes about 1.5 cm apart along the outer edge. Then make a second row further in, placing each hole between the holes of the outer row. Be careful not to punch holes on fold lines. Repeat for the remaining star points.

7 Trace the enlarged holding card pattern on the screenboard and cut out the four pieces. Make the cut in the top or bottom of each.

ASSEMBLING THE STAR

8 Put together the five Points A first. Take one, fold up the long tabs in the bottom 'V' and place the untabbed edge of the second point on the tabs. Take the cover off the tape and press the points together. Take the cover off the small tabs and press them on the second point. Repeat for the three other star Points A. Place Points B and C on either side of the five joined Points A.

9 Take the holding card pieces. Using the slits cut in them, hook together a left and right side of the holding card. Attach them to the tabs on one outside point. Repeat at the other end.

10 Assemble the light fitting according to the manufacturer's instructions. Put the bulb into the star and use two Nalclips to clip the holding cards together, opening them slightly with a pair of pliers if necessary. They will hold the star together firmly. They can be painted with correction fluid or paint to make them less noticeable.

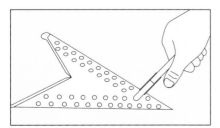

6 Punch in holes about 1.5 cm apart, making a row at the outer edge and then a second row further in.

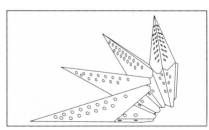

8 To put together the points fold up the tabs, take the cover off the tape and press them together one by one.

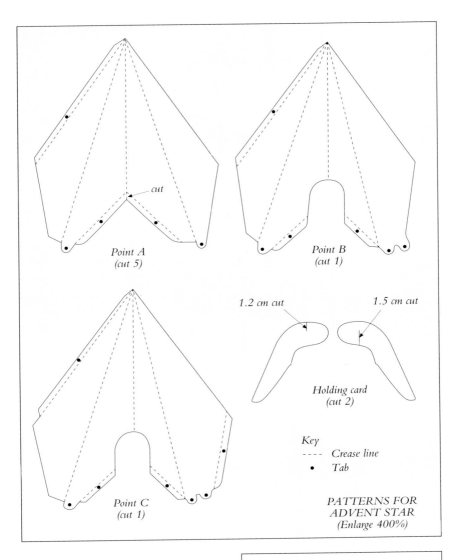

Point A
(cut 5)

cut

Point B
(cut 1)

Point C
(cut 1)

1.2 cm cut

1.5 cm cut

Holding card
(cut 2)

Key
- - - - Crease line
• Tab

PATTERNS FOR
ADVENT STAR
(Enlarge 400%)

11 Place the clips or hooks on the window frame and hang the star from the top so that all the points are free of the frame. If desired, wind ribbon or tinsel around the wire to camouflage it.

HINT

General purpose clear adhesive may be used as well as, or instead of, the double-sided tape to hold the points together.

This card holder is easy to make, decorative and useful. Make one to show off your favourite Christmas cards or make a number to display all the cards you receive. It's hinged in the middle so it folds up for easy storage.

Christmas card holder

Made from two layers of screenboard covered in seasonal fabric and glued together, this holder is a great way to display Christmas cards. Just slip a corner of each card between the two layers.

METHOD

1 The screenboard will hold the Christmas cards more securely if it is cut the correct way. To find the grain of the screenboard, take the sheet and flex it. The way it is harder to bend is across the grain; the way it is easier to bend is with the grain. Draw the patterns (see page 61) on the board so the length of each piece is across the grain. Place the board on the cutting mat and cut out the pieces with the scalpel.

2 Cut two pieces of hinge paper 5 x 16 cm for the base boards and two pieces 5 x 14 cm for the top boards. Take the top boards and lay them end to end, allowing a 5 mm gap between them. Position one piece of hinge paper under the join and the second piece on top of the

MATERIALS

- 20 cm plain fabric
- 20 cm patterned fabric
- Screenboard, 1550 UMS
- Pencil and ruler
- Cutting mat
- Scalpel
- Hinge paper (available from art shops)
- PVA adhesive
- Spreader or paint brush
- Scissors
- Spray adhesive
- Masking tape
- Awl
- 50 cm gold cord
- Tapestry needle size 18

join. Spread PVA adhesive on the boards and glue the hinge paper in place. Repeat for the base boards. You now have one hinged top board and one hinged base board.

3 Iron the fabric for the top board. Place the top board across the fabric. Cut the fabric so it fits the width of the board plus 5 cm allowance but leave the full fabric width. Cover one side of the top board with spray adhesive, wait 1 minute and then

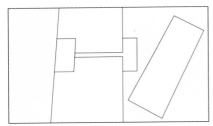

2 Lay out the top boards end to end and position one piece of hinge paper under the join and another above.

spray again. The fabric and board will adhere better with two coats. Place the board on the wrong side of the fabric. Spread PVA adhesive down the long edges of the board and fold the fabric over the edges, making sure they are neat and tight. Trim the corners and cut the fabric at the ends, leaving 5 cm allowances. Glue the fabric over the ends in the same way.

4 Follow the same steps with the base board, but be careful around the edges as 1 cm of the 'wrong' side of this board will show. Use masking tape to pull the fabric taut around the curved top.

5 Spread a generous amount of PVA adhesive down the centre of the top board, being careful not to get it on the fabric. With wrong sides facing, centre the top board on the base one. Make sure it is positioned with an even amount left around the edges.

6 Weight down the card holder with some books and leave it to dry thoroughly overnight.

7 Using the awl, make two holes in the card holder about 3 cm in from the edge and 1 cm down from the top. Thread the gold cord onto the needle and push it through the card from the front. Tie the cord together at the back for hanging.

FESTIVE FABRICS

The card holder can be made using any fabric but the red ones used give it a suitably festive appearance. If red doesn't suit your Christmas colour scheme, however, the cardholder will work equally well in other colours such as white and gold.

Small prints are easiest to position, but if you prefer large patterns choose one that is not staggered and centre it down the holder. Be careful, though, as bold prints may overwhelm the cards you're displaying.

For a co-ordinated look use matching fabric for tablecloths or napkins, or even tree decorations (use the stocking pattern on page 16 and add some braid).

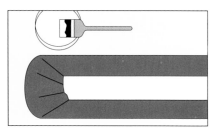

3 Fold the fabric over the long edges and cut it at top and bottom, leaving 5 cm allowances. Glue in place.

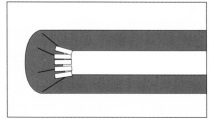

4 Use masking tape to pull the fabric taut around the top of the base board as 1 cm of the 'wrong' side will show.

Crab apple tree

Cones like these are simple to make and can be used beside a door, or as a table centrepiece or mantelpiece decoration.

MATERIALS

- 90–100 artificial crab apples
- Six branches of spruce
- Polystyrene cone, 10 cm in diameter and 25 cm high
- Artists acrylic paint: pine green
- Paint brush and scissors
- PVA glue
- Satay stick

These simple cones can look elegant or rustic depending on the base used.

METHOD

1 Paint the cone green. Cut off 3 cm long tips of spruce. Trim off a few 'leaves' at the base of the stems. Trim the crab apple stems to 3 cm with some shorter for the top of the cone.

2 One by one dip the stems into the PVA glue and push them into the cone, starting at the base. Use the satay stick to make a hole in the cone for the spruce tips. The crab apple stems are strong enough not to need a pre-made hole. Place a crab apple and spruce tip alternately. Continue up the cone until you reach the top. Fill in empty spaces with spruce tips.

3 Place the cone in an interesting container. The satay stick can be pushed into the base to support it.

1 Cut off 3 cm long tips from the spruce and trim the crab apple stems to 3 cm or shorter for the cone top.

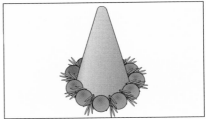

2 Dip the stems into PVA glue and push them into the cone, alternating spruce tips and crab apples.

Ribbon wreath

This beautiful wreath is composed entirely of ribbon loops pinned to a base. The technique can be adapted to any width of ribbon and, of course, any colours.

METHOD

1 Cut the blue ribbon into 40 cm lengths and the gold ribbon into 50 cm lengths.

2 Take a length of blue ribbon and fold a loop at 6 cm followed by two increasingly smaller loops. Place it at the top centre of the wreath and fix it with two pins. Make another two ribbon loops and pin them on either side, slightly lower and covering the edge of the first ribbon loop.

3 Take a length of gold ribbon. Start a fold at 7 cm, make three loops, more or less the same length, then fold the 'tail' around the loops and to the back. You should have two tails at the back and three loops at the front. Pin this ribbon loop on the wreath base at the inner edge.

MATERIALS

- Plastic-backed dry wreath base 25 cm in diameter
- One reel of 4 cm wide blue organza ribbon with satin edge
- 9 m of 8 mm wide gold ribbon
- Scissors and pins
- Wire and hook (for hanging)

4 The next gold ribbon loop will be placed on the outer edge. Place them wider apart on the outer edge, but closer together on the inner edge as you work around the wreath.

5 Continue folding and pinning the ribbons until you come full circle. Keep looking at the wreath so you get an even and pleasing result.

6 Hang the wreath on the wall.

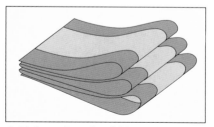

2 Take a length of blue ribbon and fold a loop at 6 cm followed by two increasingly smaller loops.

3 In the gold ribbon make three loops the same length, then fold the 'tail' around the loops and to the back.

A ribbon wreath can add a touch of luxury to your Christmas decor. For the best effect choose ribbons that give an impression of richness: those with deep colours and satin or organza finishes.

All the elements of this table are easy and quick to make but they combine to produce a lovely result. To make the gold stars scattered over the tablecloth follow the instructions on page 9.

White and gold table

These white and gold table decorations will ensure an elegant setting for Christmas dinner. Bonbons made from Unruyshi, a cut-out paper table runner and gold-sprayed angel place cards are the basic elements.

WHITE AND GOLD BONBONS

MATERIALS (FOR 12)

- White Unruyshi with gold thread
- 9.60 m of 3 mm wide white/gold ribbon
- Fourteen cardboard toilet rolls
- Scalpel
- Masking tape
- Scissors
- Twelve sheets of A5 paper (or six sheets of A4 cut in half)
- Double-sided tape
- Twelve snaps
- Trinkets

1 Cut down the length of one toilet roll. Overlap the edges until the roll is 3 cm in diameter. Use masking tape to tape the sides together and then around the roll. Repeat on the remaining rolls.

2 Cut the sheet of Unruyshi into four pieces, each 32 x 47 cm. Cut a decorative edge on the paper.

3 Lay out one piece of Unruyshi and place the A5 sheet on top of it (the A5 paper provides support as Unruyshi paper is so soft). Put the double-sided tape across the width of the paper at the other end and remove the tape cover. Place the snap on the A5 paper, and then place the prepared roll beside it. Place a trinket or treat in the roll. Place a toilet roll at either end of the prepared roll. Roll up neatly from

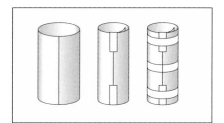

1 Make a roll 3 cm in diameter. Use masking tape to tape the sides together and then around the roll.

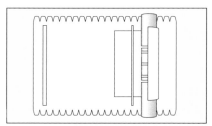

3 Lay out one piece of Unruyshi and on it place the A5 sheet, the snap, prepared roll and two other rolls.

Continue the theme with gold angel or star charms as bonbon trinkets.

A paper runner with cut-out design will dress up a plain tablecloth.

the snap end and secure at the top end with the double-sided tape.

4 Cut two pieces of ribbon 35 cm long. Take one and place it 9 cm from the edge of the roll. Move the outer toilet roll slightly but do not remove it at this stage. Overlap the ribbon and pull very tightly, then tie the ribbon and make a bow. Remove the outer toilet roll. Repeat at the other end of the bonbon, being careful to tie the ribbon the same distance in from the end so that the bonbon looks symmetrical.

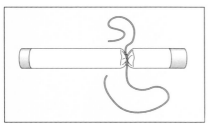

4 Place ribbon 9 cm from the edge of the roll and tie tightly around the paper between the toilet rolls.

TABLE RUNNER

MATERIALS
• Roll of white wrapping paper
• Scissors
• Blu-Tack
• Scalpel
• Cutting mat
• One-hole puncher
• Decorative-edged scissors

1 Enlarge the design on page 61 by 200 per cent and make an extra copy (you'll need two copies).

2 Cut the paper to the length needed for your table.

3 Fold the paper in half, lengthwise, then in half again.

4 Place the copy of the design in the centre of the folded paper about 15 cm from the edge. Hold it in place with Blu-Tack.

The angel can hold a place card or a name can be written on the skirt.

5 Put a new blade in the scalpel. Place the folded paper on the cutting mat and cut out the design through the copy and the wrapping paper.

6 Place the hole puncher through the centre of the star design and punch the holes in the design.

7 Remove the copy. Cut along the ends of the runner with the decorative-edged scissors.

8 Repeat the pattern at the other end of the paper.

ANGEL NAME CARDS

MATERIALS
- White card, 165 g
- Gold spray paint
- Pencil and tracing paper
- Small pair of scissors
- Pen

1 Enlarge the pattern on page 62 by 125 per cent. Using the pencil, trace the pattern onto the tracing paper and then transfer it to the wrong side of the card.

2 With a small pair of scissors cut out the circular shape. Then cut on the inside lines.

3 Spray paint the card on both sides. Allow to dry.

4 Write the name on the skirt with the pen or place a small name card in the 'arms'.

5 Assemble the angel by placing cut line A into cut line B. Fold the 'arms' down and forward.

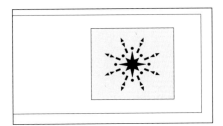

4 Place the design in the centre of the folded paper, 15 cm from the edge, and hold it in place with Blu-Tack.

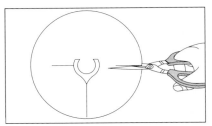

2 With a small pair of scissors cut out the circular shape. Then cut on the inside lines.

Christmas cheer table

Jewel-like colours are combined with gold to produce this exciting Christmas table. The bonbons are made from crepe paper, while beaded monograms and wired cord napkin rings complete the projects.

CREPE PAPER BONBONS

MATERIALS (FOR 12)

- Crepe paper: red, yellow and purple
- Ribbon to match, 70 cm for each bonbon
- Fourteen cardboard toilet rolls
- Scalpel
- Masking tape
- Scissors
- Double-sided tape
- Twelve snaps
- Trinkets

METHOD

1 Cut down the length of one toilet roll. Overlap the edges until the roll is 3 cm in diameter. Use masking tape to tape the sides together and then tape around the roll (see page 53). Repeat on the remaining rolls.

2 Cut a piece of crepe paper 35 cm long. Fold in each side 10 cm. Trim the corner from the folded paper on each side of one end only. Place a piece of double-sided tape across the end of the crepe paper between the cut corners.

3 Place the snap on the paper towards the other end, and then place the prepared toilet roll beside it. Place a trinket or treat in the toilet roll. Place a toilet roll at either end of the prepared roll. Remove the cover from the double-sided tape. Roll up the bonbon neatly from the snap end and secure at the top end with the double-sided tape.

HINT

The first step towards creating a successful Christmas table is to establish a theme and maintain it so there is overall consistency in your decorations. Here jewel-like colours were the unifying theme, on page 52 it was heavenly angels and stars in gold and white.

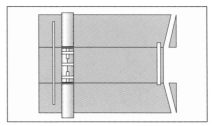

3 Place the snap on the paper towards the end, with the prepared roll beside it. Place a toilet roll at either end.

The rich colours used to decorate this table will help make a cheerful atmosphere for your Christmas celebrations. Use coloured glassware and china to complete the effect.

The ends of these bonbons are teased out to give a flower-like effect.

4 Cut two pieces of ribbon 35 cm long. Take one and place it 8 cm from the edge of the roll. Move the outer roll slightly but do not remove it at this stage. Overlap the ribbon and pull very tightly, then tie and make a bow. Remove the outer toilet roll. Repeat at the other end of the bonbon, being careful to tie the ribbon the same distance in from the end so that the finished bonbon will look symmetrical.

5 Tease out the crepe paper gently around the edge at both ends to make a flower-like shape.

MONOGRAM PLACE MARKERS

MATERIALS

- Seed beads, gold
- 14 inch (35.5 cm) long 24-gauge wires
- Round-nosed pliers
- Wire cutters
- Gold paint (optional)

1 Enlarge the monogram alphabet on page 62 by 400 per cent on the photocopier (200 per cent twice).

2 Take a length of wire and make a small loop at one end of the wire with the pliers.

3 Thread the seed beads on from the other end until you have a threaded length long enough to bend into the initial you want to make. Place the beaded wire on the initial and bend

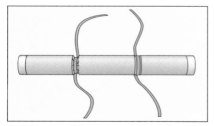

4 Place a ribbon 8 cm from the edge of the roll, tie tightly around the crepe paper between the rolls.

3 Thread the seed beads until you have a threaded length long enough to bend into the initial you want.

it to shape, looping it tightly around itself where the chart shows a solid circle. Cut the wire 1 cm from the last bead and end the initial by making a small loop in the wire with the pliers.

4 If the letter is made from two pieces of beaded wire, follow the same method, looping the additional piece tightly around the main wire as shown on the chart with a solid circle.

5 If you have used a silver wire, give the initial a neat finish by covering the ends with a little gold paint.

NAPKIN RINGS

MATERIALS

- 35 cm of wired cord for each loop
- Wire cutters or an old pair of scissors
- Adhesive tape
- PVA glue
- Two end caps for each loop

1 Cut 35 cm of cord and tape tightly around the ends. Hold one end 4 cm from the end and take the other end

1 Hold one end and take the other end around and above it and back down through the loop.

A wire loop makes a simple yet effective napkin ring, especially when combined with a beaded monogram place marker.

around and above it and back down through the loop as you would to tie a knot. Pull so the ends are even.

2 Place a little PVA glue at each end and twist on the caps. Wipe off excess glue.

3 Separate the ends slightly and press down a little on the knot. The napkin bow will stand by itself.

HINT

A colourful table looks festive but for the best effect combine no more than three colours. Other combinations would be the traditional red, green and gold, or you could try bright pink, turquoise and yellow, or even pink, blue and green.

Patterns

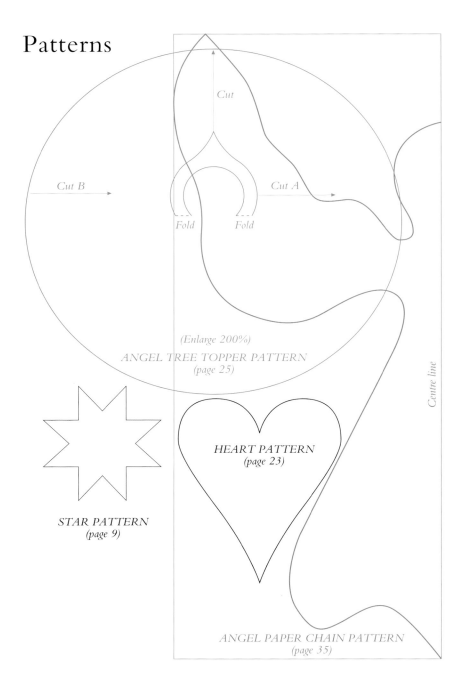

Cut

Cut B →

Cut A →

Fold   *Fold*

(Enlarge 200%)
ANGEL TREE TOPPER PATTERN
(page 25)

Centre line

HEART PATTERN
(page 23)

STAR PATTERN
(page 9)

ANGEL PAPER CHAIN PATTERN
(page 35)

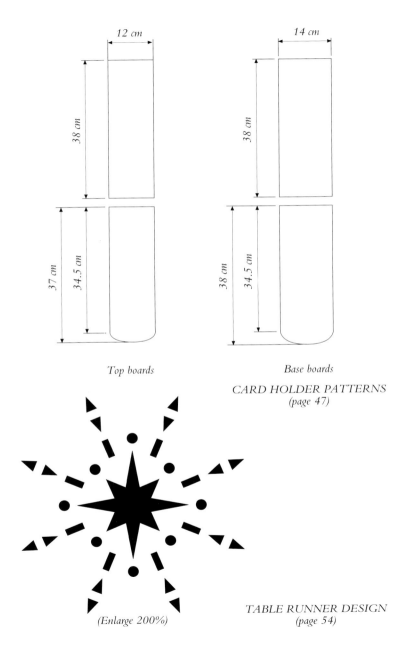

12 cm

38 cm

37 cm

34.5 cm

14 cm

38 cm

38 cm

34.5 cm

Top boards

Base boards

CARD HOLDER PATTERNS
(page 47)

(Enlarge 200%)

TABLE RUNNER DESIGN
(page 54)

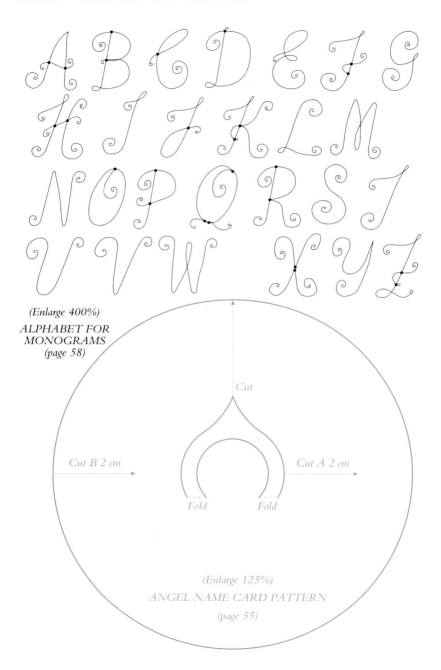

(Enlarge 400%)

*ALPHABET FOR
MONOGRAMS
(page 58)*

Cut

Cut B 2 cm

Cut A 2 cm

Fold

Fold

(Enlarge 125%)

ANGEL NAME CARD PATTERN

(page 55)

Tools for Christmas crafts

Some of the most useful tools for making the projects in this book are shown below. Most of the tools can be purchased from your local hardware or variety store.

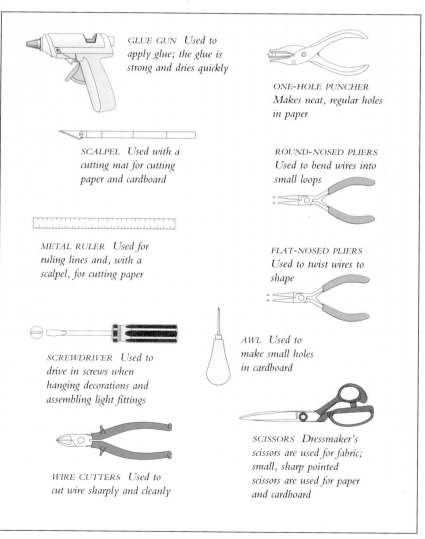

GLUE GUN *Used to apply glue; the glue is strong and dries quickly*

ONE-HOLE PUNCHER *Makes neat, regular holes in paper*

SCALPEL *Used with a cutting mat for cutting paper and cardboard*

ROUND-NOSED PLIERS *Used to bend wires into small loops*

METAL RULER *Used for ruling lines and, with a scalpel, for cutting paper*

FLAT-NOSED PLIERS *Used to twist wires to shape*

SCREWDRIVER *Used to drive in screws when hanging decorations and assembling light fittings*

AWL *Used to make small holes in cardboard*

WIRE CUTTERS *Used to cut wire sharply and cleanly*

SCISSORS *Dressmaker's scissors are used for fabric; small, sharp pointed scissors are used for paper and cardboard*

Index